SandCastle 3

Long Vowels

Aā

Mary Elizabeth Salzmann

ABDO
Publishing Company

Published by SandCastle™, an imprint of ABDO Publishing Company, 4940 Viking Drive, Edina, Minnesota 55435.

Printed in the United States.

Cover and Interior Photo credits: Comstock, Corel, Digital Stock, Photodisc

Library of Congress Cataloging-in-Publication Data

Salzmann, Mary Elizabeth, 1968-
    Aa / Mary Elizabeth Salzmann.
      p. cm. -- (Long vowels)
    Includes index.
    ISBN 1-57765-413-7
    1. Readers (Primary) [1. English language--Phonetics.] I. Title.

PE1119 .S23422 2000
428.1--dc21

00-033211

The SandCastle concept, content, and reading method have been reviewed and approved by a national advisory board including literacy specialists, librarians, elementary school teachers, early childhood education professionals, and parents.

## Let Us Know

After reading the book, SandCastle would like you to tell us your stories about reading. What is your favorite page? Was there something hard that you needed help with? Share the ups and downs of learning to read. We want to hear from you! To get posted on the Abdo Publishing Company Web site, send us email at:

**sandcastle@abdopub.com**

# About SandCastle™

## Nonfiction books for the beginning reader

- Basic concepts of phonics are incorporated with integrated language methods of reading instruction. Most words are short, and phrases, letter sounds, and word sounds are repeated.

- Readability is determined by the number of words in each sentence, the number of characters in each word, and word lists based on curriculum frameworks.

- Full-color photography reinforces word meanings and concepts.

- "Words I Can Read" list at the end of each book teaches basic elements of grammar, helps the reader recognize the words in the text, and builds vocabulary.

- Reading levels are indicated by the number of flags on the castle.

## Look for more SandCastle books in these three reading levels:

| **Level 1**<br>(one flag) | **Level 2**<br>(two flags) | **Level 3**<br>(three flags) |
|:---:|:---:|:---:|
|  |  |  |
| **Grades Pre-K to K**<br>5 or fewer words per page | **Grades K to 1**<br>5 to 10 words per page | **Grades 1 to 2**<br>10 to 15 words per page |

Here are some fun ways
to spend the day.

Do you want to play?

Ada takes care of her baby brother.

Ada is a good baby-sitter.

Adie is sitting on a bale of hay.

The hayride is about to start.

Ady is winning the race.

Jane is close behind her.

Amy has a whale named Amos.

She takes Amos to the beach.

We press our faces to
our plates for the
Jell-O-eating game.

It tastes great!

Our Rollerblades make skating fun.

Our helmets and knee pads make skating safe.

17

Abe plays in the spray
to cool off on a hot day.

19

Abel is up to bat at home plate.

What game is he playing?

(baseball)

# Words I Can Read

## Nouns

A noun is a person, place, or thing

**baby-sitter** (BAY-bee–sit-ur) p. 7
**bale** (BALE) p. 9
**baseball** (BAYSS-bawl) p. 21
**beach** (BEECH) p. 13
**brother** (BRUTH-ur) p. 7
**care** (KAIR) p. 7

**day** (DAY) pp. 5, 19
**faces** (FAYSS-ez) p. 15
**game** (GAME) pp. 15, 21
**hay** (HAY) p. 9
**hayride** (HAY-ride) p. 9
**helmets** (HEL-mitss) p. 17

**home plate** (HOME PLAYT) p. 21
**knee pads** (NEE padz) p. 17
**plates** (PLAYTSS) p. 15
**race** (RAYSS) p. 11
**spray** (SPRAY) p. 19
**ways** (WAYZ) p. 5
**whale** (WALE) p. 13

## Proper Nouns

A proper noun is the name of a person, place, or thing

**Abe** (AYB) p. 19
**Abel** (AY-buhl) p. 21
**Ada** (AY-duh) p. 7

**Adie** (AY-dee) p. 9
**Ady** (AY-dee) p. 11
**Amos** (AY-muhss) p. 13

**Amy** (AY-mee) p. 13
**Jane** (JAYN) p. 11
**Rollerblades** (ROH-lur-blaydz) p. 17

## Pronouns

A pronoun is a word that replaces a noun

**he** (HEE) p. 21
**her** (HUR) p. 11
**it** (IT) p. 15

**she** (SHEE) p. 13
**we** (WEE) p. 15
**what** (WUHT) p. 21

**you** (YOO) p. 5

22

# Verbs

## A verb is an action or being word

are (AR) p. 5
bat (BAT) p. 21
cool (KOOL) p. 19
do (DOO) p. 5
has (HAZ) p. 13
is (IZ) pp. 7, 9, 11, 21
make (MAKE) p. 17
named (NAYMD) p. 13

play (PLAY) p. 5
playing (PLAY-ing)
  p. 21
plays (PLAYZ) p. 19
press (PRESS) p. 15
sitting (SIT-ing) p. 9
skating (SKAYT-ing)
  p. 17

spend (SPEND) p. 5
start (START) p. 9
takes (TAYKSS)
  pp. 7, 13
tastes (TAYSTSS) p. 15
want (WONT) p. 5
winning (WIN-ing)
  p. 11

# Adjectives

## An adjective describes something

baby (BAY-bee) p. 7
close (CLOHSS) p. 11
fun (FUHN) pp. 5, 17
good (GUD) p. 7
great (GRAYT) p. 15

her (HUR) p. 7
hot (HOT) p. 19
Jell-O-eating (JEL–oh–
  eet-ing) p. 15
our (AR) pp. 15, 17

safe (SAYF) p. 17
some (SUHM) p. 5
up (UHP) p. 21

# Adverbs

## An adverb tells how, when, or where something happens

about (uh-BOUT) p. 9     off (AWF) p. 19

23

# Glossary

**baby-sitter** – Someone who is paid to take care of children.

**bale** – A large bundle of things tied together.

**hayride** – When a group of people rides in a wagon filled with hay.

**whale** – A large sea animal that looks like a fish but breathes air.

## More Aā Words

| | | |
|---|---|---|
| age | date | nature |
| airplane | escape | paper |
| ape | favor | radio |
| ate | gate | space |
| brave | lake | table |
| chase | mane | wave |